I Can't Find You a Boyfriend
or your keys

by
Bob Buchanan

Cover design by Vinnie Corbo
Author photo by Jessica Buchanan
Cover photo by Bob Buchanan
Back cover photo #1 by Brendon Hoke
Back cover photo #2 by Natalya Rodriguez
Edited by Cathleen O'Connor

Volossal
Publishing

Published by Volossal Publishing
www.volossal.com

Copyright © 2020
ISBN 978-1-7350184-4-7

Table of Contents

Foreward

Hello. My name is Brenda. I met Bob about three years ago through a mutual friend. I had lost my 19-year-old son in our house fire on May 4th, 2015. I was in a very bad place. I still am most of the time as there's really no getting over losing a child.

Our mutual friend told Bob she had a friend who needed help and Bob told her to have me call him, so I did. We chatted for a bit and scheduled another phone conversation. He was amazing. Not only did he know things he couldn't have, he was very kind. He was very caring.
That was the day that I learned about "the window." Bob described everything in my living room where I was sitting. I asked how he could do that, and he told me my son opened a window so he could see through it. I had no words. It was a very long conversation and Bob said he would like to meet me, so we set up a day for him to come to my home. Bob didn't know anything about that day I lost my son and everything I've ever owned. He asked me to tell him nothing and I didn't.

I was very emotional that day and Bob had my son, my father, my grandfather, and my brother all together. I was so happy Ronny was with them. Bob described everything in my home that burned down that day and said he saw firefighters there, so he knew there was a fire. He said Ronny was telling him it was just an accident and I was nearly hysterical. Bob was very confused about why I wasn't getting any comfort from this and I couldn't tell him, because he asked me not to provide any information. All I could do is cry.

He just didn't understand what was wrong with me so I told him I have to tell him so he could understand. I told him that for sixteen months I've blamed myself for the fire. When I came back to my house from the hospital the firemen were still there and there were detectives there also. One of the firefighters who brought my son out died the following day from a heart attack. I started up my front steps and he crouched down to tell me I couldn't go in. I said it's ok. It's my house. But he said I couldn't go in. I looked at a man next to me and started crying. I told him I left my son at the hospital because he wouldn't wake up and he was dirty and needed a shower, so I was going back to the hospital to get him soon. I guess I lit a cigarette and he saw I was a smoker. I found out they blamed me for starting the fire.

The fire department said the cause of the fire was unknown, but our insurance company had a fire investigator there and he told my husband that the fire started in an outlet on the side of the couch. I had to meet with a detective and my husband was meeting with different people but keeping it from me. They were telling my husband that all four firefighters who got my son out were suing me for negligence. Two firefighters got hurt bringing my son out, but they had preexisting injuries. When Bob heard this, he was stunned. He closed his eyes and was quiet for a little bit.

He told me a movie played for him and he could see the flames shooting out of the outlet. He described the entire room. Where the furniture was. Everything. I felt like a weight had been lifted off of me, but I just couldn't speak. That was a bonding experience for Bob and me that day. After sitting and just talking to each other I walked Bob out to his car where we talked some more. He told me he had been questioning his purpose in life. I couldn't believe it.

After meeting with me and seeing what I've been dealing with for sixteen months and how he helped me, saved me, I think at that moment he knew. People need him. He's a gift.

It was very emotional and spiritual. We were brought together for a reason. Bob calls me and I call him. He still keeps me on my feet when I need help. I have PTSD so sometimes I just can't deal with the loss on my own. I have many more stories to share between me and Bob. When Bob met my husband, he was getting messages from Ronny. He was saying Ronny was playing a movie for him and he was rolling around in the dirt. My husband and I about died.

We knew exactly what he saw because we have the video! Ronny was in the backyard making a video of himself on his phone. I didn't know that at the time so all I saw was Ronny rolling around in the backyard and he looked like he was dodging something. When Ronny showed me the video, he made he had inserted robots that were trying to blast him with weapons. It was so funny. I showed Bob the video and that's what Ronny sent to him to tell us. He knew it would make us laugh. And it did.

I was blessed the day I met Bob. I can talk to my son. I know he's still with me. Missing him is the hardest part. Bob reassures me. There is only one way to describe him. He's a gift.

- Brenda

Preface

The reason I titled this book *I Can't Find You a Boyfriend or Your Keys* is because it's not what I do. I am often asked this. It is common that many feel they can only be complete in a relationship. My answer to the question of "will I ever find a boyfriend or girlfriend" is usually, "when you fix yourself."

I have always known that the heart wants what it wants, and when many fall in love their eyes no longer see clearly. It will not matter what I say to someone in love unless I am telling them what they want to hear. Otherwise, they will not listen.

All too often my experience has been one where I see my client is in a bad relationship with someone not suited for them or their mate is just not a good person. If I attempt to tell them what I am seeing even after they ask, it isn't good; they do not want to hear it. They dismiss the messages and refuse to believe the souls. They feel the souls do not know what they are talking about and reject the messages out of hand, remaining in the bad relationship.

More often than not it will cause the client to walk off and never come back or worse, badmouth me to others, accusing me of not knowing what I am talking about, even after they get their messages. We need strength and exercise free will in many aspects of our life. The messages from the souls are like those from strong parents. They want us to have self-control when it comes to relationships. I hear this frequently from the souls. Yes, they guide us, but we ultimately do what we want, and get important lessons along the way.

I often receive a call from a client months, perhaps years, later who is upset the mate we spoke about is treating them bad, whether they are cheating or was just so self-centered it just didn't work out. My best advice to clients is to see people for who they are, not who we want them to be, which is tough for many.

At the same time, I encourage them not to sour on all relationships because of one individual. When we allow that to happen, we can sabotage relationships before giving them a chance; we must have a balance in all things in life. Sometimes, clients, angry with me because I told them it wasn't going to work, will stay in a bad relationship to prove I was wrong. Doing what I do is not about right or wrong. It's about getting my client to where they need to be in life. This isn't about me or my ego. The messages are to assist them to open their eyes to what the relationship is, and possibly move toward a better, happier life.

At times the message is that they can fix things, if they wish, by changing themselves. That is why I might tell them that they won't meet that boyfriend or girlfriend until they fix themselves. How that goes depends upon the person I am with, but this is why I avoid giving my messages from the souls about relationships; often, it's just a no-win situation.

As a caulbearer my messages go beyond finding you a boyfriend or your keys, although I do get that at times. It isn't what I do; I am here to help others to a better place. Having a boyfriend or a girlfriend doesn't always lead you to happiness. Happiness is up to you, only you, no one else.

The stories I tell in this book relate not to the entire session only something that took place in actual real-time. The messages come through me from beyond and, for the most part, do not stay with me. I have always wondered why, when talking about a special session, I cannot remember what was brought through, only something that took place during that session. It could be a bird showing up, a fox, or a light going on or off. The reason, I now realize, is because when something occurs here, it is in the physical reality, or as I like to say, the here and now. This is the reason it is more front and center in my memory than the messages from beyond.

Now for the keys. I can't find my own, enough said.

- Bob Buchanan

Introduction

Some are born with a "silver spoon in their mouth."
Me? I was born with a veil. The veil complicated my life
and I was often bewildered by things that happened to me.
My life started out in a good place but changed suddenly
and unexpectedly when I was sixteen, and my dad died on
December twenty-third, just a few days before Christmas. I
woke at 8:00 am with a knowing feeling. I knew something
horrible had happened to my dad. The hospital called us at
8:30 to let us know he had passed away at 8:00. That life-
changing occurrence caused me to block or attempt to block
this gift because this gift scared the hell out of me. I was
never able to differentiate if the voices I heard, or thought I
heard, were the ones I should listen to; if they were real or
my own voice of worry.

Dad was an alcoholic. As a navigator in a B17 he flew
missions over Germany. His plane was shot down on the
very first mission but he went on to fly another thirty-four
combat missions. He was troubled but, like most, he never
spoke about it; he kept it to himself. Dad was always joking
around; he used his sense of humor to get him through.

He was loved by everyone he came into contact with, both family and friends. He was a great dad. I was lucky to have had him. He was a positive and important influence on how I am today. He taught me to stand tall in the face of adversity, to never back down, and to find a solution to make things better. I always followed this when I was a cop, and I was confronted by many tense difficult situations. I was able to keep my head and think things through before acting.

A co-worker, who grew up with my wife. once told her when they were responding to a man with a gun at the apartments where we lived, "We need Bob back. He would go into a bad situation and come out with his arm around the guy like they were going for coffee." I never thought about that. I just did what I did, but that statement has stayed with me to this day some thirty-plus years later.

That is important as a caulbearer. There are times I get attacked for doing what I do by religious groups, individuals, and others who do not believe in what I do. It would be very easy to lose my cool when that happens. I rationalize it as they are entitled to their beliefs and understand they need their religion or beliefs to keep themselves centered.

Getting back to the silver spoon thing, I have never been one to live through others or envy them. I have always lived life as best as I could making do within my means. I have never looked at success in the material sense. To me, success has been enjoying my life working toward what I need, or want, and that isn't much. Don't get me wrong. I like nice things; I just don't need them to make me whole. If I want something, I set my sights on it and work towards it. That being said I will not give up the joy of living in pursuit of enjoying my life. After dad died and mom being sick, I had no time for looking at others. I focused on my life and getting through it as best I could. I always move forward.

When things have gone wrong, I do what I call dance. That is figuring out how to change things up a bit and move in another direction to make life better. I don't know what it is to give up. I have never had the privilege to do that; I have had to fight even struggle throughout my life. I do that to this day, and I do not regret a moment of my life. I have been blessed with this gift to help others. That is satisfying to me. I have to speak the truth the souls give me. When I get souls, they are with me to give my clients what they need to hear not what they want to hear. The souls never tell me how much they love my client. I feel when someone, who does what I do, tells their client, mom is here and she loves you so much, it's a way to get the client to drop their guard. I could be wrong, I just never do it. Please be careful of comments like that and make sure you don't open up, giving more information about yourself then you should.

The few souls I get are there because they love or care about my client. I was with a client who hires metaphysical providers often. She has several spiritual advisors and I was not sure why she had me come over. She has worked with past life regressionists, and several psychics and mediums. Too many, in my opinion.

I sit down and start, and her mom and dad come through. I tell her who is with us and, first thing, she says, "I know they are apologizing for the way they treated me, they always do."

My response was, "No, you need to apologize to them."

She looked at me and softly said, "you're right."

The point is, everyone else told her they were there to apologize to her because that was the obvious statement if you looked at her current situation. She was sick. However, I told her she wasn't sick, and I didn't know why she thought she was. It was at that point she told me about the others. It's the reason I do not let anyone tell me anything until I hear from their souls on the other side and I can assure you it will not be mom or dad, saying they love you.

This woman was also told by her past life regressionist that she is living her sad life because she had to come back and pay for the way she was in a past life. I'm pretty sure if you're coming back, it's to live a better life, be a better person, and make up for that "bad past life." When I told her that she agreed that would be the case. None of us really know for sure, however, knowing the other side the way I do, it's not how I understand it works.

It surprises people that I don't usually remember the messages once a session is complete. The stories I relate here in the book are not the entire session only something significant that took place during the session. The messages come through me from beyond and they, for the most part, do not stay with me. I have always wondered why, when talking about a special session, I cannot remember what was brought through. But I do remember something that took place, like a bird showing up, a fox, or a light going on or off. The reason is because what is happening is in the physical world in the here and now. So, I remember it, whereas the messages come from the non-physical world. They come from beyond.

I live by my motto that life is a journey. If success is the big mansion on the hill, but you haven't been able to find joy or enjoy the journey, you will never enjoy the mansion once you get there. Set goals for yourself. Be determined to get there but do not develop tunnel-vision to the extent you can't find happiness in life and your journey. That sounds like I'm talking in platitudes. I am not. I live what I preach.

Always be hopeful, never hopeless.

Chapter One
Mother's Day

Each Mother's Day, there are a million people on Facebook wishing their moms a very happy Mother's Day. Mother's Day can be a mixed bag of emotions, because for some, it is not a day of happiness. If you are one of the lucky ones, it is a wonderful day.

However, we should not forget others who feel lost on this day. There are those for whom this is not a day they can celebrate. I hope I can make some sense and open people to understanding what these mothers go through. This is not meant to be a downer. Please understand that it is to help those of us who are happy to perhaps understand and lift up those who are having a tough time today.

I do sessions for many, too many, mothers who no longer have their children. This is the hardest thing a parent can live with. When I do sessions for someone who has lost a child, it takes a toll on me, because there are no words in the English language that can ease the pain of a mother who has lost a child. I am always at a loss for words as a deep pain overtakes me. The only thing I can tell someone is what I see. Children are always in the light with family, they are with us to celebrate this special day and every day. This is not conjecture, it is real. My only regret is I can't take their pain with me as I leave.

Two Mothers Who Lost Children

Recently, while doing sessions at a psychic fair, two women came to have a session with me who had lost children. When I finished my session with Margret, the second woman who had lost a daughter, we talked. Margret told me her friend was upstairs with another medium. She told me she also lost a daughter. Just as she was telling me this, her friend Kim's daughter Jodi was with me. As Jodi came in, I got a cold feeling with deep pain inside. I knew Kim wasn't going to get what she needed from the medium upstairs. I told Margret if Kim didn't get what she needed to bring Kim to me, and I would give her a few minutes.

I told Margret to tell Kim not to tell the people at the fair she was coming down or they would charge her. I also knew from Jodi that Kim wasn't getting any messages and Jodi wanted to talk to Kim. I was also being told Kim would not pay again if the session she had was bad. She wouldn't trust someone else.

About fifteen minutes later Margret came downstairs with Kim and asked if that offer was still good. I simply smiled and said, "of course" and directed Kim to my room. Within seconds Jodi was talking to me, after all, she was already with me. Jodi told me she had been sick her whole life and life for her was tough. I conveyed Jodi's messages to her mom. Kim was very appreciative and thanked me. She was very happy Jodi came through. She didn't think she would because the medium she sat with upstairs didn't get Jodi until Kim asked for her. Now, that in and of itself doesn't mean the medium wouldn't have gotten her. That happens sometimes, for some reason and I don't have an answer for it, but I know the souls want to be asked for. However, according to Kim, the medium gave her nothing more than, in her words, funeral-home-speak. The usual: she is happy she is in a good place, etc. Kim was really upset, and I didn't blame her.

Before I start a session, I tell all my clients that everyone I get is in the light, in heaven and that they are whole again. Later they may show me how they died which is more important than that they are happy. The sad thing about this is Kim went to this woman in good faith hoping to talk to Jodi. When that didn't happen, she believed all of us are fake. I restored her faith in what I do.

I am not supposed to get upset with people who are fakes, but I do. I wish people who do this because they think it's cool or are seeking attention for themselves would stop doing this. They are hurting people and that isn't right. Sadly, I will say about ninety-eight percent of people who say they have the gift, do not, and rely on the client to talk a lot. If you feel you are with someone like that, get up, take your money back and leave.

The very same is true for those who have lost their mothers. They are with you and will be watching out for you as they always have.

The Flower Petal

Sometimes I am asked to do a group session, what I call a gallery, with a family. At one session, I was with the father Chris, mom Anna and daughter Judy. Upon sitting down, Chris' father came through right away, as did Anna's mom. I was giving them the messages from the souls when my attention turned to Judy. I was hearing a little voice saying, *mommy*. As always when I hear or see a child my heart drops. A little girl came through. I asked Judy if she lost a child, hoping the answer was no. She told me yes, not her child, but a child she was very close to. I told her the child was telling me that Judy was like her mom and was very close to her. This turned out to be true.

The session was taken over by the child at this point. Another woman showed up right after her who told me she was her mom's mom who was there for her, along with the rest of the family who first showed up.

After I left the session, Chris reached out to me in a text later and we spoke quite a bit about how the child, Kelly, was happy and at peace. The next morning Kelly was with me giving me more information to relay to her grandparents and Aunt Judy. She was excited and wanted them all to know she is healthy and happy.

When I awoke the next morning at 5:15 am I went to the kitchen to grab my coffee and saw a pink flower petal in the middle of the floor. It was in great shape. It looked like an Orchid petal, but I wasn't sure. I picked it up and threw it away thinking my wife may have dropped it. When she came into the kitchen I asked her if she dropped it, and she said no but perhaps it came in on her shoe after walking the dog the night before. The petal was in too good of a shape for it to have been stepped on. I went into the other room to check my orchids, but none were missing petals.

It was a mystery. I had no idea where it could have come from, and at that hour I didn't put two and two together. It was then I realized that when I awoke at 2:00 am to get some water, there was nothing on the floor. There was no way I could have missed it, even at that hour. Now, as a skeptic, I had explored all avenues of where it would have logically come from and continued to explore how it got there when I heard Kelly's little voice say thank you. I reached out to Chris to see if a pink flower petal meant anything to him, and he said yes. He sent me a photo of Kelly when she was four wearing a pink dress and holding pink flowers. Pink was her favorite color.

Later that day I was talking to Judy at which time I conveyed to her what had happened. She also told me pink was her favorite color. When she was sick, the neighbors in their neighborhood including the local fire department all displayed pink in support of her.

Kelly had reached out to say thank you in a way only her family would know. I spent a lot of that day tearing up with the pain of bringing her through me and what she felt for her family. It is this small flower petal and a child's thank you that makes doing this worthwhile.

Appreciate and Celebrate Your Mothers

Please appreciate your mother on Mother's Day whether you are a mother who has given birth or, like Judy, mothered a special little person, their child, you will never understand who mothers are or what they go through for us.

All that being said, I hope all mothers have a happy Mother's Day. Don't let sadness overtake you. Reflect upon your life with those who are no longer here. Do not forget your children who are still with us. They need you. Stand tall against the sadness, and don't let it defeat you.

Let it, in some way, lift you. I know that is easier said than done but do everything you can to honor your life with those who are no longer with us, whether it be your mother or your child.

If your mom is still with you, celebrate her with happiness, and do not take her for granted. If she has issues, try to forgive her for one day. I know that is a lot to ask but sometimes forgiveness helps you more than anything else.

Chapter Two
Signs

I am somewhat skeptical when it comes to signs. Don't ask me why. I mean, I know everyone else gets them but when it comes to myself, it is hard for me to figure out.

The Redtail Hawk

For approximately three years I worked with a family who lost their daughter. She was murdered. I haven't written or spoken much about it because they were getting a lot of attention from the press, and I didn't want to add to their pain. I told them there was an arrest coming after about two years and, sure enough, two weeks later my phone blew up at 11:00 pm from friends and family telling me there was an arrest. When working with families of high-profile murder victims I avoid watching the news.

I went to the first day of the first trial. I was only there maybe two hours. Her mother and father asked if there was going to be a conviction. I told them I saw a party and an eventual conviction, but that there would not be a conviction this time, and I gave them the reason. I was right. There was a hung jury.

The sign came to me about one year later as I was driving in rush hour traffic. It was dark, and I was in the center lane when BAM!, something hit my windshield. It scared me and sounded like whatever had hit me was coming through my windshield. I saw an exceptionally large Redtail hawk, wings spread across the windshield blocking my view. Within a few seconds, although it felt like minutes, it flew off without losing a feather. I went back to look for it that night and the next day, and it wasn't there. I realized this was a sign that had some meaning. I looked up the meaning of hawk in the Animal Totem book which states, *keep your eyes open as there is a message coming.* However, to me, the hawk is a bird of prey, a voracious hunter.

A few days later I was driving on the Taconic Parkway South in mid-afternoon, and the daughter was with me, telling me the new trial was coming. I reached out to her parents. As I was talking to them and they were telling me the new trial is coming, another Redtail hawk came flying down, talons out, coming right at my windshield like I was a mouse it was going to grab. It almost hit the windshield like the one the other night, but then it turned at the last minute and flew off. That was the sign something was happening. I realized this was for the family of the young woman who was murdered. I relayed the message to the family that a conviction was coming this time. I went to the second trial twice. As I was sitting in the courtroom alone on the first day of the trial, I got a terribly negative defeated feeling. I wasn't sure why but, within a few minutes, the defense team walked in the courtroom. I knew this time there would be a conviction and there was. The message from the Redtail hawk was that the souls were coming for the murderer to make sure the conviction would happen, and it did.

The Chickens at the Front of the House

Signs aren't always as dramatic as a hawk flying into my windshield! Jason, Judy and Kelly called me off a referral, requesting I come to their house for a group session. Upon my arrival at the home, I noticed the driveway was muddy due to rain the day before. Concerned I would get stuck, I looked around for the place where it had the least amount of mud to park. I tell you this to emphasize I was looking around and noticed everything in the front of the house. I want to make it clear; there were absolutely no chickens to be seen anywhere.

Once in the home, we sat in the kitchen which had a large window overlooking the backyard. There were chickens in the backyard, which was not your typical backyard. This was a large backyard with a chicken coop about fifty to seventy-five yards behind the house. The chickens were walking around by the coop and fenced-in area. At no time did they come up toward the house. The chickens are there for the family to gather eggs for sale to the public and for their private use.

Our session started with a young man, Nick, coming in for Jason. Nick was Jason's friend. Nick also acknowledged the whole family with whom he was very close. Nick told me Jason attempted to help him get away from drugs and get his life together, staying with him as long as he could. The Kellys took Nick under their wing as his family life was very difficult. Sadly, Nick eventually lost his battle with drugs and passed through an overdose.

As I was talking to Nick and giving Jason the messages from him, a rooster started crowing in the front of the house. I ignored it; after all, it was an egg farm. As Nick continued with his messages for both Jason and Judy, I heard what sounded like several hens join the rooster in front of the house. As we continued with the messages, the details of Nick's sad life were becoming clear. Meanwhile, the chickens were getting louder as though they were attempting to get my attention. Well, it worked, because now I am taking notice of this clatter from the birds. When I do a session, I am in the zone and don't hear or see much other than the movie the souls play for me. I was not paying attention to the chickens until this point in the session.

Right on cue, Nick began playing a funny movie of him with chickens as a little kid. The chickens were chasing him around he was maybe eight years old. Nick knowing this session being a difficult one for Jason and Judy wanted to lighten it up and give them a laugh. It is becoming clearer at this point in the session that the chickens were there to get my attention. I told Jason and Judy about the movie and they started to laugh; Nicks intent was working. I asked if Nick was afraid of the chickens, as he had indicated to me. They told me a story about Nick receiving a chicken as a kid. Nick wasn't allowed to keep it. He was afraid of chickens and would run away from them, which meant the movie I was seeing was real and not symbolic.

Once our session was complete, however, me being the skeptic that I am, I asked Judy if it was usual for the chickens to be in front making all that noise. She told me they never go to the front. It was right after Judy's answer that Nick told me he chased them to the front of the house. It was a light moment. I knew it was Nick all along; I just needed to confirm this was an event that never happens.

Once the session was finished, the chickens quieted down and went back to the backyard and their coop, a sure sign Nick was there at the farm.

Chapter Three
Names

I let everyone know names from the other side are not my thing and, although I do not get many, I do get some every so often. I do not use the cold-reading trick; I hear an O or a B. I will say the name. I always identify the souls through appearance and what they tell me their life was like with my client when they were with us. When I do get names, it is like a breeze blowing through the room; it isn't someone telling me the name. The name could be someone here they are bringing attention to, or someone I am talking to, or perhaps someone who hasn't come through yet. I even get middle names from time to time. I tell you this because of the session I had with Katie.

Katie's Mom Showed Me Roses

I was doing a phone session with Katie, and her mom came through rather quickly. Mom was showing me the movie of Katie's life with her and showed me how Katie watched over her siblings and a little about where they are in life. She also showed me a lot of kids around Katie, which usually indicates she is a teacher. It turned out she isn't yet, but she is in school to become a teacher. Grandma joined mom along with Grandpa. Grandpa showed me horses, one in particular, it was a brown and white horse. Katie told me they used to vacation at a dude ranch upstate and that was her favorite horse. I received several other messages I do not remember as the messages come through me and I do not remember most messages I get.

When I do sessions where I am not in the home of the person I am with, sometimes the souls show me something in the house to let my client know they are with them. Katie's mom chose to show me how Katie drives, which tells me mom is in the car with her often as she drives.

Then mom shows me a crystal Vase with a large bouquet of beautiful roses. First, she shows me they are on a credenza in the hallway. I asked Katie if she had roses in her home and she told me no. Next, her mom shows me them on a table in the living room in mom's home; again no. Suddenly, mom is moving these roses all over and laughing; she is a playful soul. I began to realize the roses were being used as a message for me. As I was about to ask Katie if her mom or someone is named Rose, Katie told me her middle name is Rose.

Mom picked a unique way of giving me Katie's middle name. My gifts are always changing. I never know what is next, but this kind of thing keeps me on my toes. Katie was very happy with her messages and when my client is happy, I find it very fulfilling.

Scott, Dad's Dog

Sometimes the names surprise me. I was doing a phone session with Ilene. Ilene's mom, dad, sister, mom's mom and brother all came through with incredible energy. I did get three names for Ilene. I remember getting Peter, who was on the other side. He was an uncle she was close to. He came through at the end after I heard his name. The other name was her brother's daughter, who is here and is close to Ilene. He told me how close Ilene and she are. To be honest, I do not remember the name but I'm pretty sure it was Kathleen.

I remember little about the sessions. Again, those who are clients and follow me, know this. Then I heard Scott, but it wasn't like most names. Ilene's dad was telling me the name, but it didn't come through like the normal breeze I hear names in.

Up until this point her brother was very strong. He was the one who had just passed, and the soul Ilene was closest to. It turned out hearing Scott was dad's way of bringing attention back to himself.

I asked Ilene if she knew a Scott, and she said the only Scott she knew was her dad's dog or a distant relative. As she was telling me who the human Scott was, her voice trailed off in my mind, and if you can visualize this, it was like Ilene went from being on the phone talking to me to hearing her falling away from me. I just didn't hear who that relative was, letting me know it wasn't the person. It was at this point I decided to let go of the dog as well, because I don't get pets, but as I said, the distant relative was not resonating for me. I asked dad which one it was, he told me it's his dog. I wasn't accepting the dog when all of a sudden, he played a strong movie for me of him and Scott, his dog, walking down a rural road carrying a stick. I saw Scott as a smaller brown and white dog.

At this point, I told dad if this made sense to Ilene, I would accept it. After explaining the scene, I was seeing to Ilene. She laughed and confirmed what I saw as real. Dad was very close to Scott. Hearing what Ilene told me, I had to accept the movie as meaningful for Ilene which it absolutely was. The movie was a warm loving movie, and it was meaningful not just for Ilene, but for me as well, making me aware my gifts are changing.

The Young Boy

I can be very hard on myself. I was booked for a party to meet with people individually for thirty minutes each.

The original plan was for four people; I prefer no more than eight. However, when I arrived, my client allowed more to come than originally booked, and we had a total of fourteen. Because I do not like to disappoint people, I agreed to allow everyone to sit with me.

The first woman in was a young woman. As the souls came in for her, a young boy came bounding in smiling. He was around ten years old. I asked her if she knew this kid who passed, and she told me no. We continued, but the boy stayed, and I asked her a few more times if she knew who he was. She said no, so I ignored him. The boy was still with me when the next woman came in. I asked her if he was for her; she also said no. He faded in the background but didn't leave.

Several others came down for their sessions, but I didn't ask about him. I was thinking maybe he was from the area or something. What I do isn't perfect. It wasn't until another young woman came in that he came forward again. I wasn't going to ask her but because he came forward, I asked if she knew him. She also said no. At this point I realized he liked the young girls and was a bit mischievous.

Finally, toward the end, two women came in together. Kim and Pam were the tenth clients. At this point, I was getting tired, as I had also done two intense private sessions during the day in Rockland. This young boy came forward again, but I chose to ignore him as he had shown up too often. I was giving Kim and Pam their messages. It was a bit hard because this kid just kept standing there. I never thought to ask them if he was for them.

After Kim and Pam received messages, Kim stopped me and said we are here for a specific reason. She told me they were here looking for Pam's son who was killed in an accident. I told them, or perhaps asked if the boy I had with me was her son. She said it sounded like him.

I explained the situation and how he was with me all night. I know I gave them some messages but as usual, I cannot remember them. I was extremely disappointed in myself for not paying attention, and also because I allowed the friend to say exactly why they were there. I tell people if someone hasn't come through, just give me a name and don't tell me who he is, they will come through. I must have not said that to them.

I felt I let the mother down. I take what I do very seriously and when I miss something, it hurts me perhaps more than the person I am with. I always get messages for others; I have never left anyone without getting anything, but I always want more for my client. This boy, Steven, has stayed with me from time to time he will make come to me but doesn't say anything and I felt bad his mom would never hear what he had to say. I felt she would not come back to me after letting her down.

Several months later, Pam reached out to me to book an appointment with her and her husband Dan at their home. Well, Steven came through very strong. They both got messages that were meaningful, but one I can remember clearly is Steven showed me him sneaking up on his mother and throwing a black rubber spider at her to scare her. Both Pam and Dan laughed because he would do that often. As I was leaving and they were walking me out, Dan stopped, pointed to the ceiling, smiled, and said, "look." On the ceiling was a black spider. Steven still has his sense of humor and I am glad I was able to give them his messages.

Chapter Four
It's Not Easy for Me

People assume that those who are healers or help others are free of the trials life brings with it. The healers, as I will refer to them, could be Doctors or medical personnel, even lawyers. police or firefighters who are called upon to help others in this life. We all face the same challenges; it is how we deal with them that makes us different from one another. Some believe that because I have these special gifts, I don't endure hardships in my life. The truth is we are not immune to difficulty in life.

At this time in my life, I am going through a very tough time financially. I keep my prices low so people who need messages can afford me and there are situations where people are in a very bad place where I do not charge them. I have never made this about money; it has always been about spirituality. I am thankful that my difficulties are only financial. I know I can work to overcome them but, at this point in my life, I had hoped to be in a better place. I have worked since I was fourteen; I have never had it easy.

Eagle Lake, Maine

There was a time when I was in a better place and making money until circumstances beyond my control changed things. In short, my life has been a rollercoaster ride and I have always endured and overcome. Recently the pressure became overwhelming. I felt defeated and hopeless. I was walking my dog when I lost it and began yelling at God. *Please stop, please give me the strength I need to continue. Please, I need some sort of financial relief.*

I was fed up, depressed, angry, and done being a caulbearer. Yes, I knew I would have to live with these gifts whether I shared them or not. When I got home, I was getting ready to do my self-hypnosis as I laid down, I told myself I was done, and I would put more energy into my photography business. I felt this had no purpose, I made no difference in people's lives. I wasn't sure about the messages I got and me being me, I always want more. I just never accept the fact the souls give me the messages they want you to hear. I always ask them for more, but I get what they want me to have period.

I lay down and start my journey. My panacea is Eagle Lake Maine. I leave the cabin to go down the stairs, get in a boat, say hello to the moose that is always there, I have no idea why. The moose is quite ninety-nine percent of the time but when he speaks there is always a reason. He said to me, "you have to get going."

I always get in a boat and head up the lake. I step onto shore by a small stream and begin my walk through the woods up to the top of the mountain which overlooks a beautiful wooded valley.

Not this time. This time I step onshore and I am in a deep fog. I was afraid to move onto the dangerous terrain. Suddenly I hear a soft voice say, "keep walking." I say "I can't it's too dangerous." The soft voices said, "keep walking you will be ok". I follow the direction of the voice and keep walking. The next thing I know I am at the mountain top. This time it's a desert valley with what looks like thousands of people. I am not sure if they are symbolic of people here or past. The soft voice tells me, "You can't stop doing this. See these people, they are the people you are here to help."

The phone rang and took me out of my vision. Being a skeptic, the next day I said to myself, if that was my imagination, I will be able to get back there and see if there was a message in all this. Well, I went back stepped on land, and it was clear as usual. I heard the soft voice again, telling me, "believe what happened yesterday." I was confused but figured I should consider following the directions of the voice. I planned to not continue on my Caul journey, yet I was going to be open to the message, even though I still wasn't sure it was real or imagined.

Cathy's Message to Me

About two weeks later, I was doing sessions at a party with seven women who were getting 30-minute appointments each. The second to the last woman, Cathy, is standing up when we finished. She sits back down looks at me, and says, "you can't stop doing this." I was surprised and asked her if I said anything about that to her? She said, "No, I don't know why I said that."

I have seen Cathy several times since then. We speak about it and she has no reason why she said that; it just came to her (I think she has some of the gifts). I knew this was a very strong sign, and the answer to my questions because I was preparing for this to be my last interaction with people as a caul.

By the way, within days of my temper tantrum with God, my phone started to ring, and I got very busy... Coincidence? I doubt it. Thank you God; I am forever grateful.

Chapter Five
The Souls Guide Us

Many who come to me seek information about their future. They want to know if they are going to be successful at one thing or another. It is completely up to the souls if I see that. At times I see something will work for my client. I have seen a successful career at writing, art, and a book. However, this isn't always the case; there is no way to control what I get. I am cautious because what I see doesn't always happen, at least not in the time frame my client would like.

I am only capable of hearing what the souls want me to hear and, although I hear you can be successful from time to time at whatever it is you are seeking, it's up to you, my client, to do the work. The souls will give me messages on where they want you to go or where you can go but it is very important to understand when souls give us a message that you are headed in the right direction and how to get you started in the right direction if you are to achieve your success. This isn't permission for you to sit back and wait for the souls to do it for you.

The souls can only guide us. Yes, they will influence what happens in our lives by closing or opening doors. We should keep in mind no matter what the message, we cannot wait for something to happen. It is up to you to do the work necessary to get what you want out of life. We have free will and we have to understand and respect that.

Simply said, what happens in our lives, is up to us to make happen. Take the hope you get from the message and push forward. The souls will be behind you pointing the way. Do not expect it to be easy. It can be a hard road, more often than not, so stay with it and keep going.

As you do so, keep an open mind. Realize as thing progress that you may be moving in a different direction you had hoped to move. If that happens just go with it; see where you end up. Learn to dance as I call it. Never give up; never get discouraged. The souls will be guiding you the whole way.

It is up to us to make our lives what they are. Only you can change things, provided you never give up. I know this because sometimes the souls have to remind me that this is as true for me as it is for my clients.

Fran Capo

Fran Capo who is the world's fastest talking woman, comedian, author and so much more, gave me a call. She tells me we met maybe five years ago at a Yorktown Chamber of Commerce meeting. I was on the board at the time and engaged in conversation with many people so I couldn't place her. I gave her my card and never thought about it again.

When Fran called, she told me we spoke but neither of us remembered what the conversation was about. Once I told her I was a caulbearer who has written a book, *They Speak Through me, Messages from Beyond*, she was interested in having me on her podcast to talk about my book and what I do as a caulbearer.

Before she had me on, she wanted to make sure I was real as there are just too many people who claim to do what I do sadly just are not real. During the phone interview,

Fran's mom and dad came through. At one point her dad was telling me he was proud of William's accomplishment. Fran couldn't place a William and told me the name makes no sense. Now, names not being my thing I let it go.

She liked her messages and we set up a one on one. Upon arriving at her house, she advised me when she told her husband Steve about the call, he reminded her William is her son. The reason she didn't get it is that they call William by his middle name Spencer. Spencer, unbeknownst to his mom, went to college and got his degree as a surprise to her. You may feel this doesn't make sense, but it isn't uncommon for me to give my client something that makes sense the next day, week, or month.

Fran is an author of many books, one is called, *Hopeville*, a voice she believed to be a Divine spirit was telling her this story and she wrote it in one day. She gave me the book which is about a village that had lost all hope until an angel appeared and gave everyone a candle. The light of the candle was hope and they were told the more hope they had, the brighter it would burn.

At this point in my life, I was struggling with having hope. People believe I'm always in a good place, but this just isn't so. No matter how hard I tried to get out of this funk I couldn't. The message in this book was powerful for me and began my journey back to where I need to be. Fran's book was exactly what I needed. I believe the messages Frans received were what she needed as well.

Fran and I did a fifteen-minute podcast and you can get the links for the podcast and her book on my Facebook page (address in last chapter). I can't thank Fran enough for the opportunity to be on her podcast and giving me her book. I know I was guided by the souls to that opportunity and to receiving the message I so needed to get at that point in my life.

Chapter Six
Relationships

There are no humans without flaws of either sex. When getting into any relationship you have to recognize what those flaws are and decide if you can live with them. Sadly, you might accept a person who is just not good believing you can or will change them. If that is how you think, you are taking a big chance. More often than not, you cannot change another person. Narcissism, being abusive, passive-aggressive, and self-centered are not flaws; they are beyond that. They are character issues that are psychological. It depends upon your definition of flaws. But beware of a man bearing flowers on the first date who does everything right. Being a guy, and knowing many guys....well, just saying.

Some people don't know how to be happy. I believe those who consistently complain are happy complaining. Many don't understand a very basic rule: look at the person you are dating with practical eyes and see them for who they are not who you think they are or who you want them to be.

Without Trust, There is No Love

Where there is no trust, there is no life. Where there is no trust, there is only suffocation. Where there is no trust there is no joy. Where there is no trust one can only exist, not live. Where there is no trust there can never be love. Where there is no trust, happiness cannot exist. It is impossible. Without trust, there is no joy to life just existence and that is no way to live life. If you can't trust another, it can be all-consuming. If you lack trust without reason, fix yourself. If you lack trust and there is a good reason, leave. Living that life of mistrust prevents nothing from happening except perhaps the joys in life that will be missed.

If someone makes a misstep you have two choices, forgive and let it go or not forgive. If you can't let it go, you are now down to one choice. You have to leave so the both of you can get on with your lives. I recommend people go into any relationship with open eyes. Be realistic. Never want anything so badly you refuse to see the truth. The truth is not what you want it to be; the truth is what it is. Having a mate doesn't bring instant happiness and can make you very unhappy in the long run if you get into a relationship with someone who is seriously flawed. There are good relationships, but I want you to know how you can avoid the bad relationship and find the right one for you.

Soulmates

I am often asked by my client if I can see if they will meet their soulmate, will I find a relationship, or why can't I find someone. The bottom line is we don't have all the answers The souls often don't come to me with those types of answers. So when I say I can't find you a boyfriend or your keys which I consider a carnival act, it's not me who can't see that information, it's the souls who don't want to give me, or I believe anyone, that information.

My answer to finding you a mate is more often than not, "when you fix yourself." The souls want us to exercise free will and self-control, the bottom line is the souls expect us to deal with life on our own. When it comes to relationships they will only assist you with them. I hear this frequently from the souls and I have to respect what they give me.

Clients who come to see me who ask questions about finding a mate can't expect us to get that answer. We may but that isn't something you should seek out from the souls. This is something most legit people who do what I do, do not like to answer. There is rarely an answer to this question from the other side; we know that but we will ask for you anyway.

No one walks the face of this earth who is without flaws, no one. We have to acknowledge our flaws and if necessary change if we can. That being said, we have to be who we are and cannot be who we think the person of our desires wants us to be, be yourself if they like that person the relationship will happen if not you will be better off in the long one run.

Some of us simply expect too much when it comes to relationships. We somehow have reached the point that we feel others should adjust to our needs, or be the person we want them to be, not the person they are. We must see our partner for who they are and either accept them as is or if you can't live with those flaws or traits move on. At the beginning of a relationship, we don't see who our partner is, we see our partner as being who we want them to be, or in some cases, we look for what's wrong with them.

To have a healthy relationship, we need to be open to discussions about what bothers you and see if a change can come about. The most important thing is never, repeat never consistently point out your partner's flaws, which will destroy a relationship faster than anything else.

There was a series on TV called *Dirty John*, based on a true story about a woman who fell for a psychopath. No one, especially her children, liked him. When they found out who he really was she dismissed it, and refused to believe anything negative about him, accusing them of being jealous and thinking he was just after her money. I tell you this story because I can't begin to tell you how many come to me regarding their relationship and if I tell them that person, man or woman isn't good, they ignore the advice, refuse to believe it, and move forward with the relationship. It is sad how often the advice from the souls is spot on and is ignored.

Some want the relationship to work so badly they ignore the souls' messages and stay in denial until they can no longer ignore the truth. When I give them what I hear, or am being told, they refuse to hear or believe what I tell them. I turn into the bad guy and I lose the client. No matter. I refuse to tell my clients what they want to hear; I stay with the messages from the souls.

Joan Couldn't Accept the Truth about Paul

My client Joan wanted to know about Paul, a man she had been seeing. Joan attempted to control the conversation by telling me what a great family man Paul was. She told me I should see him with his nephews, and then I would know. Joan was certain she was going to have a lasting relationship with Paul. I stuck with the souls who told me Paul was no good. When I conveyed this to Joan, she admitted Paul had done time twice for very serious crimes.

She continued asking me questions about him, again, attempting to control the conversation. Finally, to prove me wrong she pushed Paul about getting more serious. It was at this point Paul admitted to Joan that he was seeing three other women beside her and that he was "pretty much" (I'm not sure what that means) using her. Joan blew up, threw him out of her life, and told him to never come back.

About a week later Joan calls me to ask if Paul will come back into her life. I told her no, the same message I had been getting all along. She really didn't like that message and refused to accept it. She kept asking me the same questions about Paul and refused to believe the messages. When I told her, her souls would no longer address her relationship with Paul, as they always do if you keep rejecting their messages, she got very angry.

She insisted I gave her conflicting messages. I did not. She heard the messages as conflicting. She told me I told her she would have a relationship with Paul, and it would be wonderful. No, what I told her was she would have a relationship with him if she pushed but it would never be what she wanted. What she heard was "you will have a wonderful relationship with him someday." I finally told her to not come back to me because she became verbally abusive and attacked me on every level.

She got upset that I wouldn't entertain her or her souls any longer, but when someone is abusive and refuses to accept the souls' messages, I need to walk away. I have no idea if Paul ever came back into her life or not. I get "the feeling" he never did. She went from recommending me to bad mouthing me. I will have to live with that and overcome it if I can.

Now you know why I resist working on relationships. I am sure I have had some success with them, but I just can't remember. Perhaps the best answer to will you ever find a relationship is that it's all up to you. The point to all this is that happiness is up to you. Work on your own life and stop looking for a relationship to make you happy.

Frankie

Frankie's mom Carla called me telling me she is worried about him because he is not in a good place.

I immediately heard the soft voice telling me Frankie was considering suicide. I told that to Carla who freaked out because she had been a client and knows how accurate I was with her. I told her she needs to get him help or I would see him too see if I could reach him.

A few days later Frankie called to set up an appointment. We met in a parking lot of a Dunkin Donuts in New Rochelle. Frankie is a tough kid and had an attitude about this. He only showed up for his mother who insisted he come to see me. He got out of his car and leaned against it, arms folded. He was saying through his attitude, *ok I'm here. lay your B.S. on me and I'll be on my way.* His grandfather, a very strong soul, was with me before his arrival giving me messages.

I didn't even do my opening about how it works for me. I got right into Frankie's face pointed at him and said with a stern fast voice, "You're sitting in your room crying. You are going to your grandfather's grave asking him if it's ok to come to him." I told Frankie it's not ok; he has to stay here.

With that Frankie's face changed, his arm dropped, and he looked stunned and shook his head yes. Frankie's messages continued for over an hour. He was getting a lot about a recent breakup. Because he was in such a bad place over the breakup, we continued to do support sessions and spoke on the phone every night either text or voice until I was able to reach him. It took over a year.

Frankie's engagement was ended by his fiancé. It took a lot of time and hard work, but I reached Frankie by being honest and telling him exactly who she was. His fiancé was also not in a good place. I explained to him who she was and what he missed. Frankie resisted when he got messages about her and their relationship. Like most people Frankie wanted to hear what he wanted to hear; he was hoping for a Hallmark moment where she would come running back to him and they would live happily ever after. I have to tell people what the souls want you to hear not what you want to hear.

It is my work with Frankie that is one of the reasons I do not like to do relationships. I have at least two others who I gave messages to who not only have chosen to ignore the messages but try to prove me wrong. They also stop coming to me when they don't get those messages, which I am fine with. I don't like, nor do I want, to give messages that people refuse to believe. Honestly, there is no ego here, so I hope my messages I give them are wrong for their sake at times. I can only give people what I hear not what they want to hear.

Frankie's initial session was over six years ago; we still talk and have become friends. Frankie still breaks my chops about how right on the message was. He is also very supportive; he gets me and knows how I often question myself. It turns out everything I told him was true. He resisted many of the messages about the relationship. He did his best to prove me wrong, not in a malicious way. Like many, he just wanted what he wanted. I appreciate and understand why people do it because perhaps things can be wrong we don't have all the answers. Although that is rare, if ever.

We have free will but I do hope people keep an open mind about the messages they get and proceed with at least caution.

Frankie is the perfect example of the heart wanting what the heart wants. Too often when it comes to matters of the heart clients attempt to control the messages. That is a waste of time, with me at least. I can't speak for others.

Chapter Seven
Electronic Messages

Sometimes the souls communicate or let me know of their presence using electronics. I was doing a session for Mary. I was getting her father, who she spoke with every day, maybe a few times a day while he was here. She validated that and was getting very emotional telling me that, if she were in a place where she needed support, he was there for her. He was her rock.

Her father was showing me a phone, and he said he was contacting her on the phone. I asked her if that was happening. She said, no, it wasn't. I told her to keep an eye out for texts that made no sense, or maybe whispering on a phone call with someone else. These are all things that both my clients and I have experienced directly.

As we are in the middle of talking about this, my phone rings, I never answer my phone during a session, the phone number coming up was 000-000-0000. Now, this is the second time this has happened during a session. I didn't answer as I thought it may be a telemarketer. There was no message left and I went on.

After the session I began to question this and regretted not picking up the phone. Later that evening the phone rang again with the same number. I answered it thinking it would be a telemarketer. No one was on the other end. I waited but no one spoke. Then, all of a sudden, I heard whispers I couldn't make out. It was the same whispers I have heard before from the other side.

I can't, for certain, attest to the fact it was her father or someone for me. I simply can't be sure what it was, but one thing I know is that it wasn't a telemarketer, at least not from this side. And it wasn't the first time it happened.

Lucy and the Walkie-Talkie

The souls can communicate through other electronic devices as Lucy's mom, Anna did. I was sitting with Lucy doing a session. It was Lucy, me, and her infant son who was sleeping in a carrier sitting on the floor next to her. Lucy has recently lost her mother Anna, who she was very close to. As the session started, Anna came in along with Lucy's grandmother. mother-in-law and a few other souls. Anna was playing the movie of her life with Lucy. She included another short movie acknowledging her sons, Lucy's brothers, who are still on this side.

About fifty minutes into our session, Anna showed me a phone. When I see this the souls are telling me that they spoke with the person I am with often, usually every day, even several times a day. However, this time Anna was telling me she is using the phone to try to communicate with her loved ones.

I told Lucy what Anna said, I continued to explain to Lucy how this could happen and what to be aware of, such as voices that sound like whispers on the phone, or perhaps the phone rings and no one is there. I explained how twice I got a call from phone number 000-000-0000 during sessions, and how, when I answer, no one is there. I just know it is the soul we are speaking with at the time.

I told Lucy she also may hear static. Just as I was saying that a walkie talkie, sitting on the couch not far from Lucy, went off and we heard static. It was two short bursts like someone was trying to talk to us. We were both startled.

Lucy picked up on it immediately as did I. She grabbed the Walkie Talkie and asked if I heard that, which I had. It was crazy and the timing was incredible.

Being the skeptic that I am, I stopped and look at all possibilities. There was no one else in the home as I said. Nothing was running in the home. No appliances. Nothing. There was nothing that caused the Walkie Talkie to act up. There was nothing in the air. I never knew it was there the whole time because it was so quiet. Because of the timing, I knew it was Anna letting us know she was with us.

I still asked, "Anna, is that you?" She started to laugh and said what do you think? With that statement and the way she said it, with a little laugh, I had no doubt it was Anna talking to Lucy.

Joann's Mom was Singing on the Phone

During a phone session with Joann, her mother and grandmother came to me. Joann had just lost her mother, who was her best friend; they did everything together. Her mother wanted to reassure Joann she was whole again (something I know happens and get often). She played the movie of some of the highlights of their life together. Grandma was also with us giving Joann comfort and letting us know she and Joann's mom are together. I was at the point in the session where they were opening up the window on Joann's life. Grandma was showing me that Joann was experiencing a great deal of sadness and sorrow, more than normal. Mom told me that, since her passing, Joann has been feeling extremely lonely.

I was addressing this with Joann when suddenly we began to hear singing on the phone. It was a woman's voice, and I paused for a moment to listen to see if I could find where the signing was coming from. I pulled my ear away from the phone to listen to make sure it wasn't coming from outside, a TV or radio, but it was not coming from outside. Just to confirm it was on the phone and not coming from outside, I asked Joann if she was playing music. She confirmed she was not. At this point, I am doubting the singing is on the phone.

I always check all possibilities of what it is I am experiencing. I question: Is it from the other side? Is it something going on here (on this side), I may have missed? I want to be positive and convince myself in incidences such as this, leaving no doubt about what is happening.

Once I was sure it was on the phone, I asked Joann if she heard the signing as well. She confirmed she was hearing it, but it didn't sound as clear to her as it did to me. The singing was very soft and sounded a bit different but, clearly, it was a woman's voice. It didn't sound like someone here was singing; it sounded like it was coming from the other side.

Once I was sure it was one of the souls for Joann, I informed her of that. This was all happening so fast I was trying to sort things out. It was at this point where Joann told me her mom would always sing to her when she was feeling sad and lonely.

You may be wondering why I didn't see her singing in the movie she showed me. The reason was that, as the singing began, the movie stopped playing. Why? I have no idea. Sometimes things just happen the way they are meant to; there isn't always an explanation.

Joann needed something to bring her comfort, and her mom knew just what she needed to lift her spirits at that moment. The souls always do.

Chapter Eight
Honoring My Process and My Time

There are many misconceptions about this modality and what happens. I understand how this occurs as many who do what I do put out a mystical concept, or should I say misconceptions about how this works. You should always apply logic to this and everything in life. One misconception, often promoted by TV personalities, is that we get messages anywhere and anytime. That may be true for some, however, that is not how I work.

I need to concentrate, focus if you will, and go into a zone. Yes, on occasion I will get something without going into the zone, but that is rare. It usually happens when I have people who have suffered an extreme loss such as the death of a child or parent who was very close to my client. Those of us who do this work are not perfect nor do we have all the answers, another misconception.

Client Calls at the Last Minute

I have always understood and accepted this is how it works for me. Recently, I became painfully aware of how people have a belief in how it works and do not truly understand. I received a text message from a now-former client, accusing me of no longer having the gift. She texted that I am only about the money because she called me last minute and wanted me to see her and I could not, I have to concentrate and prepare, but she could not accept that.

This particular client made several appointments she did not keep. Then, several weeks later on a Saturday, she text-messaged me and asked if I work weekends. I responded, yes, but only Saturdays. A few minutes later she asks if I am around. This was about 2:45 pm and I was driving upstate to meet with friends. I wrote back, saying no I'm busy. Perhaps, I should have chosen my words better, but I was being honest.

A week or so later I get another message from her, saying how she no longer believes in me because I should have known she was in a bad place and I should have seen her. She texts, "Instead, you told me you were busy, that is not what mediums do."

Let's look at what took place that day. I was driving, and she never asked if I was free or available, just if I was around Yorktown. I couldn't focus because I was driving. In her mind, I should have known and turned around to meet with her because in her words "that is what mediums do."

The truth is we are human and have lives outside of this work. Most people who reach out will tell me they are in a bad way in some way. If I am talking to them on the phone I may feel that but when it comes to electronic media, I just can't connect that well, if at all. Especially if I am doing something like driving and can't open up. Perhaps, had she kept one of the other appointments she made, she would not have attacked me as she did.

This event made it clear to me that others have to respect my time. I needed this to happen as it brought awareness that I often drop things to attempt to accommodate my clients. It is okay not to do that.

Joe Wanted to Know what Kathy Said to Him

People come to me with the preconceived idea of how I work or expecting to hear what they want to hear. We don't have all the answers as some believe we do. I can only hear what the souls want me to know. Yes, we can sometimes push them into telling us things you want to hear but the messages they come with are the messages you need to hear. They will not let you down, provided you are open-minded. When someone is cynical, untrusting, and angry and seeks validation of the messages they get from other mediums or psychics, it doesn't work, for me or the souls. We need to respect the souls. I show them respect through accepting the information they want me to hear. I will ask the souls questions without pushing too hard which often works.

Another client, Joe, did a phone session with me. He was condescending, obnoxious and being a jerk throughout the session. He received many messages, all of which he confirmed. When we came to the end of the session he said, "Bob, you have been one hundred percent on, however"... (I love that *however*) "I will believe you if you can tell me what Kathy, my wife, said to me when she got mad."

This was after a long session where he received quite a few messages that were all correct according to him. He heard things I could not have guessed or known. Sadly, Joe wanted to validate our session and his messages beyond what he got. When we were finished Joe again said, "Bob you are one hundred percent correct, but I will not believe you unless you tell me what Kathy would say to me when she was mad at me."

This type of challenge is taken by the souls as not believing in them. They will give me answers but not always. This upsets the souls, but I asked Kathy what she would have said. She told me, "this old fool does this all the time. He's nasty to me then wants me to give him what he wants?" It did not come through in the session, she was confiding this to me. Joe wasn't nice to her in life, but she didn't take his crap. Well, she wouldn't tell me the answer. This happens more often than I would like. Although, on one occasion I had a soul, a client Bob's daughter, tell me what Bob wanted to hear. I wrote about this in my book, *They Speak Through Me, Messages from Beyond* (Chapter 6, Page 63).

Anyway, back to Joe. His wife refused to give me the answer. When I told this to Joe, he took off on me telling me about a medium who was much better than I was, he got names etcetera. I happen to be friends with the medium he was hitting me over the head with. Yes, he gets a lot of names and dates but not much more. I also gave Joe messages on how he could work through things that my friend doesn't do. He is one of the very good ones that I trust. You get the picture of who I was dealing with.

Well, the next morning as I woke up, Kathy came back and gave me the answer to Joe's question. "Drop Dead and Go to Hell," she laughed. I reached out to the woman who knew them and told her. She confirmed this and asked if I was going to call him and tell him. I told her no; I wasn't going to subject myself to his abusive ways. Like with Joe's wife Kathy, there are times when a soul from a session will come back to me a day or maybe a week later and give me more information. I will reach out to my client and more often than not the message is meaningful.

Chapter Nine
Messages After I Leave My Client

Like with Joe's wife Kathy, there are times when a soul from a session will come back to me a day or maybe a week later and give me more information. I will reach out to my client and more often than not the message is meaningful.

I was Sitting in Lisa's Father-in-Law's Seat

I went to see Lisa, and when our session was almost over, she asked for her father-in-law. He came through and gave me messages for her. The next day he came back, breaking my chops about me sitting in his seat while I was there. Lisa and I had met downstairs in what looked to me to be a room for entertaining. Unfortunately, I didn't put my client's phone number into her appointment so I can't contact her and will not know if it's true. I have no idea if that message would make sense to Lisa or not, but the way I heard it, I believe it had some meaning.

The Cross

Sometimes the souls don't want to overload my client and will give me more later. For the record, I do not bring my beliefs into my sessions in any respect. I do not have that right and do not judge others. I do know of many who do let personal beliefs bleed into their readings. I believe allowing that to happen is unethical, selfish, and egotistical – none of which belongs in a session.

When I do a session, I am in a zone and am connected to the souls and my client. I watch the black and white movie the souls play and try to make sense of it. If I let my personal feelings come into our session, the messages will not be accurate. My personal beliefs or feelings are not why clients come to me. I say this because this story can be looked at as controversial. I hope it isn't. It is not meant to be. What I am about to tell you is what exactly happened.

During a session with a group, one of the women, Elaina, was wearing a small cross. My attention kept going to the cross. It was lighting up, as I like to say. Even with that, I was not getting messages about the cross at that time. I do not do what I call the carnival act and ask did your mother or father give you that or is that your grandmother's kind of thing. I just continued giving her the messages I was getting for her. Once Elaina received her messages I moved on to the next person.

A few days later as I was driving a Grandmother was with me showing me that cross again. I had forgotten about it and wasn't sure who was wearing it. Sharon, one of the participants from the group, happened to call me just after Grandma's short visit. I asked her if she wore the cross, and she told me Elaina was wearing it.

I realized Elaina's grandmother was the one who came to me. The reason for the visit was she was proud of her granddaughter and wanted Elaina to know how she felt and that she made the right decision. She told me Elaina was going to terminate her pregnancy but decide last minute not to do so.

All this came from nowhere. I wasn't thinking about her, the cross or the session. Grandma just popped in for a quick visit. I questioned the visit because of the way it came in, but

I had to check. Because Elaina was the one who set up the session, I had her number. I reached out to her via text and asked if she had a minute to talk.

She did and when I told her what I was getting she confirmed it as true. She told me it was a last-minute decision to have her daughter. She was on her way to have the procedure when she made that choice. I know Grandma had a little something to do with it. She knew her granddaughter, the love and compassion she has for children. I just got that as I am writing this.

Today Elana has a beautiful baby girl who is the love of her life and is happy and grateful she made that decision. I never know when a soul will jump in on me to give me a message my client needs to hear. It doesn't happen often.

Why didn't I get that message while I was there? I have no idea why that happens. I don't have all the answers, even though some believe I should. I've learned to just go along with things as they happen and listen to the voices. I would like to say I do this without question but that is not true. I do question the souls; I simply do not always get the answers. There are things the other side does not want us to know, and I am accepting that more and more. Hell, I have no choice.

Chapter Ten
On Suicide, Communication Right After Death and Grief

I wrote about my first session with Brenda in my last book *They Speak Through Me*. I have spoken to Brenda on several occasions since then. Brenda lost her son Ronnie in a house fire in her home in 2015. A friend connected Brenda to me without saying anything more than Brenda lost her house to a house fire and she lost everything.

Recently Brenda did a video interview with me for my webpage. As we spoke, Brenda reminded me of a few things that took place during our original session. At one point in the video, Brenda mentions how I was questioning myself and wondered what purpose I serve; I had completely forgotten about that. I was in a bad place, an awfully bad place. When I saw the messages Brenda received and how they helped her, I realized that what I do helps others. Brenda's session was as important to me as it was to her. It was because of our session I am still doing this. I was planning to quit this before I met her.

Brenda reminded me after the video was shot that when we first spoke on the phone, I described her living room and was spot on. It was that phone call that let her know I was real and not someone looking to take advantage of her.

Brenda's husband, Brian, joined us after the video. It wasn't a session, but I was receiving messages. Their son, Ronnie, was with me and his two grandfathers came through to make an appearance, letting me know they are with him as well. It was just a short session. During that mini-session, Ronnie showed me a video of him doing somersaults in the backyard. Brenda and Brian just looked at each other and began to laugh. Brian told me that video is still on Brenda's phone. Ronnie was into making movies, After shooting that video of himself in the back yard, he added special effects of robots attacking from outer space.

I told Brenda that Ronnie is proud of her because she is beginning to move through things a little better. Ronnie gave both of them healing messages, and he showed me how his dad was handling this whole thing which was surprising to me and I think Brenda as well.

I have offered Brenda many support sessions which she doesn't take me up on, but today it came to light that family members feel as though she is making it about her. Nothing could be further from the truth. They both avoid holidays with the extended family because they don't want to bring them down. It was clear to me the family just wanted to be there for them, nothing more, but misunderstood why they didn't want to go.

Jennifer's Sister Passed

Several years back, when I was in a particularly bad place, a friend told me I should embrace tantra. I was not completely sure what that was, but he told me he knows someone by the name of Jennifer who specialized in Tantra massage. He assured me it would be uplifting, and I should give her a call.

I carried her number around for a week or two before calling. She told me about her services in which she received $200.00. One of my issues was income, so I thanked her for her time but told her I could not afford it. She dropped her price to $150.00. I explained what I do and that I didn't make enough to justify spending that money. I also explained to her who I am, and I couldn't accept, in good conscience, her dropping her rate. It just was not right. I felt bad that she felt she had to drop her price. I never negotiate. I don't like doing that; it's just who I am.

She later called back and told me she felt she needed to connect with me for some reason and told me we can work a trade. I said no it still wasn't right and we hung up. She asked me my rate, asking me if I could come down and do a session for her. I told her that would be possible, and we made an appointment to meet later in the month.

Several weeks later at 9:30 AM Sunday, she called me very upset. She reminded me who she was, she told me her sister had passed that morning and asked if I could give her anything about her sister. I explained at that moment I was shooting Trap in a league and couldn't do it right then, when all of a sudden, I had a woman with me. I said I have a woman about five feet, with me very pale skin, black hair, and she is dancing. She started to cry and told me that was her sister. She was a belly dancer. I don't recall the messages but one thing I told Jennifer was that her sister is whole again. She was showing us that through the dancing, a sign that two things occurred once she passed. One is she could move again, because she had lost her ability to move, and she was able to breathe again which had been difficult for her for some time before her passing.

As it turned out her sister had cancer and was very sick when I initially called her. It was very clear it wasn't about a massage for me but the messages she was going to need. Since then, Jennifer and I have become good friends. I was able to assist her to get through these difficult times, which is what I do.

We Are Not Allowed to Choose Our Time to Leave

Very often this is how things work. The souls reach out to my clients in some way and bring them to me. In this case, it was her mother who knew she would need messages soon. I often sit with people who have lost a loved one to suicide.

When it comes to suicide, this is what I see.

I am always told we are not allowed to choose our time to leave. God says when we are allowed to cross over. Anyone who leaves before their time, I see between worlds; I see them in the gray. By leaving before their time, they need forgiveness and prayers from those they have hurt in order to make it to the light.

Once someone crosses over, and this is true for all, I see them as whole again. All the ailments they suffered with here are gone. They often show me themselves as younger. That includes those who left earlier than their time.

I have spoken to a few people who have died and come back. They all tell me the same thing. They are in the light but never get to the other side and are met by a relative who looks younger and sent back. They feel the beauty, as I do, yet they just don't see it. This is on purpose, so we stay here to complete our work no matter what that work is.

We should never assume how someone is processing their loss, even if you have been there. All people are not the same and handle things differently. It's best for all that we do not judge others in this life unless you are living in their skin. That will never happen, so don't judge anyone; it's not our place to judge others.

I do not do this to bring attention to myself. I do it because this is my calling and what I have been chosen to do.

Chapter Eleven
House Clearings

I have done several house clearings, almost all presences were relatives of the people in the house just letting them know they are there for them. There are a lot of myths around this. I have never gotten evil from the other side and I am sure evil goes to the dark once they cross over and never comes out.

Guns Falling off the Racks

I was called to a sporting goods store where I was shown a video of three guns falling off the rack. This should not have happened as the guns were leaning back. I sat with the owner of the store, Jessica, and her mother Carol, and concentrated. Jessica's grandfather, Carol's dad came through. I described the soul, Joe, his height and their relationship with him when he was here. They confirmed it was him. I asked Joe why he did that and why only three guns? He told me all three belonged to the same guy who treated Jessica very badly. Grandpa also told me the store took them in on consignment to sell; Jessica confirmed that. Grandpa told me the guy was a misogynist and was disrespectful to Jessica. They confirmed this, as well.

Grandpa told Jessica to get rid of the guns and all would be good. They did, and nothing has happened since.

The Man Who Loved Children

I was called to a house in New Jersey where two women, Cathy and Mary, mother and daughter, were concerned about things going on downstairs where the children played, and one child slept. As I concentrated on who was there, a gentleman who loved children and watched over them, came through to me. He told me he was there to look over the kids, but he would go down the street to a house where there were several children if he made them nervous. Cathy and Mary confirmed that the house was three doors down, but told me to tell him he can stay, seeing as how he was there for the kids. Cathy, the mother, asked if he pushed her mother down the stairs as she was claiming. He said, "no, her foot slipped off the front of the stair, but she's a bitch and he wished he did." They broke out laughing and said, "that is so true!" The soul, a harmless kind man, was from the neighborhood and loved children they told him to stay.

Dad Came at 5:00 am

Another Sunday afternoon, I received a call from Karen, who was distraught over something that happened at 5:00 am. Karen told me she heard footsteps in her bedroom that woke her up. When she looked to her left, she saw a man looking out her window. It frightened her, not knowing who this man was or what was happening. Karen did know it wasn't someone from this side and she knew she had to do something about it.

Karen got my number from the gun store owner I had helped. She gave me a call and explained how she heard the footsteps and saw this person looking out her window. I was very busy that day and told Karen I could not come but could maybe make it Monday. As it turned out, my calendar cleared that day and I was able to make it to Karen's house.

Upon arriving, we went up to her bedroom to see what I could feel. I got a revolutionary army encampment which was a bit behind the house. At first, I thought it was a soldier that was in the house but then I started to feel and hear her father. Her boyfriend, Jack, came to the house as we made our way down the stairs. We all sat in the kitchen as I began to concentrate and went into the zone.

As I concentrated, Karen's dad came in along with her mother, grandmother, and a few other souls. Karen's dad told me it was him in her room. He told me he had to get her attention and get me there so he could talk to her. Dad wasn't in her life and she always wondered why and who he was. I proceeded to tell her that her father was telling me he wasn't a good father, to say the least. He showed me his drinking issues and his anger, along with other issues he had. He told me when he was home which wasn't that often, he took his anger out on his family and Karen in particular.

He wasn't present during his time here for his family. He also told me Karen was looking to heal from her life as a young girl and the damage she suffered from living this hard life I was seeing, much of which he was a big part of. Without going into too much detail here, Dad told me Karen is in a place in her life where she was looking for answers and needed to heal from the damage he did to her. She has finally come to a place in her life where things had to change. Karen confirmed the message from her father as did Jack. Jack told me Karen talked to him a lot about this. When I looked over at Jack he looked a little surprised by how accurate the message was. I continued to bring in other souls for Karen including her mother and grandmother with messages on how she could heal.

Dad gave Karen what she needed. I don't remember exactly what her messages were as I rarely do. He did start by giving her things she could validate. Once we established that, he went on to tell what happened that caused him to leave. Karen got closure through his messages as well as the messages from mom, grandma and the others. I told Karen her dad would be around, but she would not see him again.

Aunt Mary has Messages for Jack

At one point during her session, I heard the name, Mary.

I asked Karen if she knew a Mary? Karen said no, and I said, Aunt Mary?

Again, she said no. Then her boyfriend, Jack, who wasn't a believer, said, "I think that may be for me." I turned to him and quickly said "dark hair, smoking a cigarette, playing cards?" Jack began to laugh and said, "that's her." Jack received some messages that day which were meaningful to him.

Once the session ended, I told him how I thought I may know him. I had met him years ago at a chamber event held at his place. He travels with singer Jessica Lynn and her family, who I knew, but I didn't know him.

I was very surprised he was accepting of all this. He is a Born-Again Christian. Had I known it was him I would have most likely asked him to leave or I would have left, because they are fervent in their disbelief and refuse to accept what I do. They are true skeptics, and from time to time I am attacked online by them. It was at that point I understood why I was getting the skepticism from him. He never mentioned or acknowledged that or what happened any further. By the time I was finished with his mini session he was a believer.

I advised Karen her father would remain there to help her heal from the damage of her young life but would not show himself. He only did it initially to shake her up enough to find me or someone like me, so he could give her his messages.

I texted Karen to ask if her dad showed up again, her answer, "No, all is well."

I often see Jack. He is a true believer now. He told me Karen's dad has not shown up again, as I told her he wouldn't.

When you hear something in the house move, fall off a shelf or table, do not freak out. It's a soul that is caring and either is mischievous or just wants to let you know they are there. I firmly believe the only evil or bad souls are those on TV or in the movies. If you don't want them there, just tell them to leave. They usually will, or get someone like me who can talk to them and tell them to leave, they will or perhaps they will continue to stay until you hear the message they have for you as well. You can sage, spread Holy Water, or whatever other rituals you think will help, but it usually doesn't work. Just know all is well with them being there and they mean you no harm.

Chapter Twelve
Using Psychology?

Comments on one of my Facebook posts by a woman named Sue got me thinking about how my gift developed. Sue commented on one of my posts accusing me and all who do what I do of being fakes and using psychological tricks. I realized Sue must have had a bad experience with someone, apparently a fake.

She continued to attack me, but I stayed with her, having a conversation in response to her comments, not attacking her, but defending myself. I finally asked her to talk in private and not put this on display because some of my clients started to come to my defense, which I appreciated. Sue and I spoke, and I gave her messages I was getting for her and who they were from. She couldn't believe what I was getting, as I could have never found this information on the internet. She asked how I was getting all this. I simply asked her how she thought I was getting all this. She was extremely troubled, all of which came through along with how she could get back on her feet. I would not let her give me her last name or any information about herself which is how I work. This convinced her I was real. As a caulbearer, the messages I get are more about where someone is and how to get to the other side of whatever is holding them back.

Sue and I worked together for a while, and we were making great progress getting her on her way and on the right track in her life. Sadly, she eventually fell off the map and stopped communicating.

Rockland Community College – Psych 101

Sue's initial accusations started me thinking about the psychology aspect from her point of view. She forced me to remember things long forgotten. I started questioning myself, as usual. Had I taken a psych class? Yes, I did. When I went to Rockland Community College, I took psych 101.

Something began happening while I was there. I began giving one or two of the students in my class help with their issues. Now at this point, I had approximately fifteen minutes of psych 101. I didn't have enough education to understand I was not capable of giving any advice, particularly what I was giving them. I definitely wasn't qualified in any way to be helping anyone with their issues as a psychologist. I knew this. However, the information I was giving them was spot on which confused me even more. The messages for them just flowed; they came naturally, and I was confused as to where I was getting the information. I was the one doing all the talking they never gave me any information, which confused me.

The next thing I knew I was kind of a thing on campus being sought out by many more of my fellow students which confused me even more. This was happening through word of mouth. I couldn't help but wonder what I was doing and where all this information was coming from. How was I getting all this information? The only answer I could come up with that made any sense at the time was, perhaps I am a psych prodigy? Yes, I am an over-thinker and not always rational. LOL

My psych professor, Joe Perone, heard about what was happening with me and realized he needed to talk to me. After one of his classes, he came up to me and said let's take a walk and talk. I was like, oh no this isn't going to be good.

He began telling me how the students were talking about how good I was. This confused me even more because I had no idea where the messages I had for those who sat with me came from. I didn't even think they made sense because they often didn't to me, yet they did hit home with them.

He explained to me that I needed to understand the responsibility that came with what I was doing. I told him I really didn't want all this attention and tried to avoid some of the students. He told me to do what I felt was right. He continued with good advice, telling me I had to be very careful because some of the women would find me attractive because I was there for them. Here I am a nineteen-year-old male saying to myself ... good to know.... LOL. (full disclosure, I never hit on any of the women). I continued doing this until the semester ended. I returned to college for the second semester but left quickly as I am not the school type. I never went back again.

What I do is Different

Fast forward to today, as I roll the movie of what had happened back then in my memory, reflecting on what Sue had said, I realize what was happening back then and how I was connecting to them. I now realize it was their loved ones talking to me. As I said, I have always had this gift throughout my life; I just didn't understand it. It took Sue and her comment to bring me back to those days I had long forgotten, and to bring awareness that I have been doing this longer then I realized.

When I first came out several years back I realized what I was doing was different from what the mediums I had been with did. Reflecting on how I just knew things and how the information flowed for those students cleared up why; mystery solved. Sue's interaction with me helped me to make sense about that which confused me back then. This cleared up many questions for my crazy inquisitive brain; all finally making sense.

My journey has been a long and often a mysterious one, but I'm here now. I plan on continuing on this road if that is God's will. The only joy I get from this is when I reach people and help them to get to a better place. This is not all about me or my ego. Hell, just the opposite. It's often painful, creating anxiety in me every time I go see someone. I worry I may let them down. Yet God gives me the strength to continue with the messages for others, and I have no plans of stopping.

To Sue's point about using psychology, I believe she may be right. Too many who do what I do make it all about them and their egos. I know many ask a lot of questions. It happened to me, and I wonder now how much Psych they had in school. They act as if they are cool, yet they have no idea what this is really about. If they make this about themselves, being a skeptic, I question their validity. For the record, I always question mine. It is when I give my client messages I could not have known or found on the internet, that I validate my own gift.

It turned out Sue had been to a psychic down on a boardwalk in New Jersey who was a fake. She knew it and was upset that she was scammed. I hope Sue is where she needs to be today.

Chapter Thirteen
Clients Who Need Me are Brought to Me

Knowing that what I do helps others is why I do this. The souls seem to guide those who need my help to me at the exact right time.

Kelly's Dad Sent a Butterfly

I was speaking to Kelly from Kansas who has lost her entire family. She was recommended to me by her friend. It turned out her friend, a client of mine, saw how lonely she felt and thought she would benefit by speaking to me.

As we started, her sister who she was very close to, was the first in, followed by her dad and mom. Mom and dad had a lot to say and pretty much dominated the session. Kelly's dad, with whom she was very close, told me he was very intelligent and was showing me rocket science and a science lab. Kelly was having a lot of problems in her college lab class. He was showing me how much he was helping her get through it. When I asked Kelly if she had any questions she asked if her sister had more to say.

The sister showed me many things they did together. When her sister first came in, she showed me she was a hippie, with long black curly hair. The vision of her was very clear. After Kelly's question, her sister showed me that she and Kelly had dinner often and would often take in a movie. She also showed me she was a good cook. She showed me this by showing me she was taking various foods out of a large double door refrigerator. It was a stainless-steel kitchen that looked like a restaurant even though she didn't work in a kitchen.

Kelly's sister had a dry sense of humor and jokingly told me Kelly was an awful cook, and she at one point tried to choke down a meal Kelly cooked for her. That turned out to actually have happened.

Her sister showed me a phone which is a sign they talked every day which was also true. When we were talking to her sister, Kelly's phone disconnected several times. Once I realized it was Kelly's sister and acknowledged it, we didn't lose the signal again. Finally, I saw her as a very young girl and her sister as a teenager. I saw Kelly had blond curly hair, in contrast to her sister's black curly hair.

Now, this might not sound like much more than a typical session, but the difference was I got much more detailed information for Kelly than usual. Kelly was in such a bad place missing her family, and I believe it was why I was getting so much for her.

In the end, Kelly's dad told me she will see a butterfly. I asked her if she was seeing butterflies. She said no. Dad assured me he was sending her one. The next day I received a text from Kelly advising me that she saw a butterfly. Kelly's dad told me he is a man of his word and kept his word. I reached out to Kelly to give her that message from him, and she told me he always said, "all you have is your word."

Hearing from her family helped Kelly get to a better place, which is the purpose of my messages.

Anna's Daughter Died in a Car Accident

During a phone session, a young woman came through to me to tell me she was my client Anna's daughter Maria;

she let me know she passed suddenly. I was getting a headache and saw her head hit on what looked like a window. I realized it was a car accident. Maria also told me the driver was drinking and she was the only one out of three who died in the accident.

As I was telling this to Anna she interrupted me, which I ask clients not to do, and told me a large piece of glass pierced her Maria, and that it wasn't that she hit her head. I told Anna, I'm sorry but I saw Maria hit her head. It was sudden; she didn't suffer. I told Anna, I didn't know where she got the glass piercing causing Maria's death, but I told her again what I saw. I informed Anna the vision was very strong and it's not symbolic when I see it that strong; it is what happened. Anna also validated that there were three people in the car and her Maria was the only one who passed. She also validated that the driver had been drinking.

Anna told me she went to a show put on by a very famous medium eight months back. At the end of the show, this "famous Medium" asked the audience if anyone lost someone in an accident. Anna, along with four others, raised their hands. The medium picked Anna. Anna told her that Maria died of head injuries. The medium told Anna the accident her daughter died in was a horrific accident. Aren't all accidents where someone passes horrific? The medium continued to tell Anna her Maria was pierced by a large piece of glass.

Anna told this "famous" medium that her daughter hit her head, just like I saw. The medium told her she was lied to; that it was the large piece of glass which came loose from the window that pierced Maria. The show ended on that dramatic event.

My client carried the horrific picture painted by the "famous medium" around for eight months. I firmly informed Anna I had to stay with what I saw, again telling Anna everything else I saw in that accident, the drinking and the two others living through the accident was correct. It was at this point I asked Anna what was the findings of both the police and the coroner? She informed me they told her it was a head injury that caused Maria's death. When Anna informed me of this, it again validated what I saw. I also informed Anna I strongly believed this medium no longer has her gifts, and I still have mine, so I have to go with what I saw.

The next morning Maria woke me at 5:00 am to tell me she is furious with that Famous Medium for misleading her mother and hurting her the way she did. She told me the reason for the lie about the glass was so this medium would end her show with something dramatic for her audience. I reached out to Anna to tell her this. Anna told me how much better she felt after our session. This is my real payment for what I do.

Note: I have investigated thousands of auto accidents as both a police officer and a forensic photographer. When the glass breaks, it is safety glass, and it shatters into small pieces. I have never seen large sharp pieces of glass break off like that in all my years of investigating accidents. All too often people that do what I do seem to feel they have to bring some dramatic bad news, often misleading their client. All I can think of as to why they do this is ego. This isn't about ego and ego should be left at home.

I put my sessions in the hands of God and it's working.

Chapter Fourteen
The Vision, The Firefighter –
Welcome Home Brother

I received a phone call from my sister Donna. She informed me that Chris, a client she sent me who had lost her daughter, just lost her brother. Donna told me the brother, Claren, a White Plains Firefighter had passed, and she wanted to know if Chris's daughter Erin was there to meet her uncle when he crossed.

I am very practical when it comes to this modality and told Donna that Erin was most likely there – the short answer. However, I couldn't say for sure as I rarely see that and couldn't focus on it at that time.

Erin and the Firefighters

The next morning, I woke to a beautiful image of Erin along with two firefighters greeting her uncle Claren as he crossed over. There was also what looked like hundreds of other firefighters behind her; an honor guard lining the way to Heaven for Claren. Suddenly, both Erin and Claren were with me. They began to give me some details about Claren. Claren told me he passed from a 9/11 related illness and that he had always played with the kids when they were little. I had my doubts about the 9/11 illness because he was a White

Plains firefighter, but the souls don't lie to me, so I checked with Donna.

I called Donna to tell her what my vision was and what I was told. Donna wasn't sure if any of that was true but because of what she knew of Claren, she doubted either one was true. As we were talking, the image of the firefighter came back to me very strongly. I told Donna to check to find out if any of what I heard was true. A few days later Donna called me and confirmed that Claren was at the towers and he did pass from a 9/11 related illness. Donna confirmed he did play with the kids when they were younger.

Creating My Vision

With that validation, it also validated my vision as real. I had a strong feeling pushing me to recreate my vision as best I could. I put out a call for models on Facebook and asked my nephew Brendon if he would do it. I also asked his father Rich if he would do it as well, and they both agreed. I received a call from a friend who saw my Facebook post, Rich Carrol, who connected me with Peter Campanelli who brought three others including his father who was NYFD and worked the towers that day to pose. Although a photograph could never be as beautiful as my vision, this is as close as I could get.

I can't thank those who stepped up to assist me to create this image enough, to let me, in my way, honor those who were there and paid the ultimate sacrifice or who were there selflessly risking it all to help others, everyone, believing in something.

God Bless you all.

NEVER FORGET 9/11!

Chapter Fifteen
More About Who I Am and How This Works for Me

Everyone has heard of mediums or psychics. We see them on TV. Watching a medium on TV isn't representative of the reality of this, and you may feel this is the coolest thing in the world. You would be wrong. When the provider is real and doing this right, we often feel great emotional pain, relating to our clients' pain. This is a choosing, not a choice, for those of us who are real.

As you now know, I am what is known as a caulbearer. That means I was born with a veil on my face, a physical membrane that covers the face and only the face, and which is removed by the surgeons. It is not the amniotic sac or birth sack that covers the whole body. The facial caul is extremely rare, where the birth sac is a bit more common. It is my belief that being born with the caul is a sign that we are here to use the gifts granted by God in ways they are meant to be used. We are granted different gifts. Some of us have gifts to help people in their emotional journey, while others are here to help with the physical journey. If you think this is me being conceited, believe me it is not. This is not about me at all, it is about the gifts granted to me that allow me to have tools to assist people in their darkness and to help them move to the light.

What is the Difference?

Many of us born with the veil have gifts that are said to be granted by God. Our gifts open us up to assist others through the pain in their lives as best we can. We can only guide our clients through their pain using the messages given to us from the souls who know them. However, it is up to our client to take the journey. Everyone has free will.

The souls who come to me with the messages do not have to be related to my client, but they are people who were close to my client while here on their worldly journey. I do not get many souls, just the ones closest to my client who need to give their loved ones the messages they need at the time.

My gifts vary from client to client depending upon their needs. Some get what they need through one session, others may need me to walk by their side until we get them where they need to be. I do not make this about money, and I have helped many who cannot afford the service.

At the beginning of each session, I always tell my clients how it works for me. I close my eyes and concentrate. The souls come to me in a faded black and white movie as they speak to me in whispers. This has always been the best way I know how to describe it.

The truth is I could never figure out exactly what the movie was. Although they are present, it's as though they are speaking from the other side of the room. I am sitting on one plane and they are on another just above me.

My Vision of the Skylight in Meditation

In meditation, I asked God and the divine entities to help guide me to an understanding of what it is I experience when I speak with the souls. A vision came to me in a strong concise manner. A soft voice explained what was occurring as I was shown a skylight opening at the top of my head.

I was shown that my soul travels through the skylight as I am guided to the souls. My soul, or the part of my soul that never detaches from me, travels into the light to those souls. I am invited to meet with them on the other side. I am allowed to join them; it is not me who calls them in. The only way to explain the whispers when they address me is that it's like a telephone connection. At the same time, the images and messages are being sent back to my physical being here so I can relay the messages to my client.

That vision gave me clarity as to what I see and how it works. It's not like having a conversation here. I am not allowed to go completely to the other side and see what I believe is heaven. It is my belief that anyone who has received the gift from God to do this work never sees heaven. I believe it is so beautiful we would not want to stay here.

Making a Difference is My Reward

This gift is amazing, stressful, and causes a lot of anxiety. It is often very emotional and difficult. The reward comes when I see my messages make a difference in my client's life. My ego is not invited. Be aware if someone who claims they do this makes it about themselves. They simply do not have the gift.

I hope this helps you understand who this guy is, sitting here at my computer writing this stuff, as well as what it is I do. I can't stress enough how important it is to have a healthy sense of humor to assist me to get through the pain that comes with this journey I am on. Yes, a good healthy sense of humor is important. Never lose it.

For more information about me please visit my website.
www.bobbcaulmedium.com

or on Facebook
www.facebook.com/bobbmedium